MAXWELL RENSHAW

The Breakthrough Mindset

Cultivating Resilience for Personal Success

This book was professionally typeset on Reedsy.
Find out more at reedsy.com

Contents

Foreword

In a world characterized by constant change and never before seen challenges, the ability to cultivate resilience can be your most powerful ally. "The Breakthrough Mindset: Cultivating Resilience for Personal Success" serves as an invaluable guide to transforming adversity into opportunity. Through the pages of this book, you will be strategically equipped with insights and tools to not only weather life's inevitable storms but to thrive beyond them. Drawing on thought personal experiences, real-life success stories and research, this book empowers you to unlock your inherent potential and begin on a transformative journey.

As you delve into these pages, you'll discover not just strategies for enduring hardship but actionable plans for achieving personal success. You will learn how to harness the power of a resilient mindset, turning setbacks into setups for triumph. The information here not only informs but also inspires, encouraging you to take intentional and strategic actions toward your goals with renewed confidence and clarity.

Finally, if this book has helped guide you on your path to personal success, I invite you to share your experience by leaving a review on Amazon KDP. Your insights could be the catalyst for others to begin their journey towards a resilient and fulfilled life. Thank you for beginning this transformative journey with us. May the resilience you build set the stage for your success.

1

Introduction

In a world filled with constant challenges and opportunities, the ability to bounce back and thrive is more crucial than ever. "The Breakthrough Mindset: Cultivating Resilience for Personal Success" explores the transformative power of resilience, offering you a strategic guide to unlocking your full potential. This book is designed to empower individuals by providing insightful strategies to overcome the limitations and obstacles that often hold us back. Our journey begins with the observation that many people yield too easily to setbacks, allowing self-imposed limits or external restrictions to hinder their progress. We've all experienced moments where doubt creeps in, where the paths ahead seem impenetrable. These are the instances when resilience acts as the cornerstone of success, propelling us toward our goals despite adversity. This book explains why having a strong mindset is important and how it can change both personal and professional lives. It shows how developing resilience helps us see challenges as chances to grow.

In this book you will discover a framework centered around building resilience, with its teachings rooted in real-life stories, cutting-edge research, and actionable advice. From breaking free of societal expectations to dispelling the myths of fixed limitations, this book provides a roadmap to nurturing mental fortitude. Delving into disciplines such as positive psychology, the power of will, and persistent actions, we will explore practical strategies to enhance resilience, ensuring its impact extends beyond temporary motivational boosts to create lasting change.

The decision to write this book originated from a personal journey of realization. From my earliest memories, I have been fueled by a persistent drive to push boundaries, never settling for anything less than giving 110% effort in every endeavour I undertook. Possible, sometimes more than that, because somehow, I have always wanted to be a superhuman. This lifelong habit, a compulsion almost, has driven me through countless challenges and accomplishments. Yet, it was resilience – this intangible, yet profoundly tangible force – that emerged as the true champion in my life's journey. Resilience became my silent partner, instilling within me an unyielding belief that with sheer willpower, anything is possible. Time and time again, when life threw obstacles my way, it was resilience that allowed me to rise, adapt, and move forward, empowering me to rewrite the story of my struggles into sagas of victory.

As I reflect on my path, however, I recognize that possessing resilience and willpower is only part of the equation. For many years, my energy was indeed boundless, but it was not always directed purposefully. In numerous instances, I found myself pushing hard against barriers that neither required my full attention nor aligned with my true aspirations. This misalignment taught me an valuable lesson: the significance of focusing efforts on the right things. Understanding how to harness resilience as a guiding compass, I began to channel my energy more strategically toward goals that resonated with my deepest values. Today, my journey is far from over. Each day presents new challenges and uncharted territories to explore with resilience lighting the way. I continue to refine my focus, learning to adjust my course as needed to ensure I am making meaningful progress toward my vision of success. In sharing this book, my hope is to connect with you on a personal level, offering insights that resonate with your own experiences and aspirations. Together, we can embrace the transformative potential of resilience, pushing beyond the limits of our perceived possibilities and achieving more than we ever dared to dream.

This topic is not just an interesting sideline; it's an urgent imperative. In an era defined by rapid technological advancements, economic fluctuations, and personal pressures, resilience equips us to adapt, innovate, and lead. The stakes have never been higher—our success in navigating life's trials hinges on our resilience. Everyone should care deeply about this subject because it directly influences their capacity to achieve personal fulfilment and professional prowess, carving pathways to success that might otherwise seem unreachable.

In "The Breakthrough Mindset: Cultivating Resilience for Personal Success," you'll find more than just tales of triumph. You'll uncover an empowering blueprint to transform setbacks into springboards, dismantle self-imposed barriers, and lead a resilient life marked by continuous growth and achievement. As you delve deeper into these pages, prepare to begin a journey of relentless possibility, armed with the insights and strategies that will redefine how you approach challenges and chart a course toward success.

2

Understanding Resilience as a Pathway to Success

Resilience serves as the bedrock on which individuals build enduring success in both personal and professional realms. As opposed to merely surviving adversity, resilience is about thriving through it, turning challenges into opportunities for growth and renewal. The foundation of resilience lies in our ability to understand and harness the complex interplay of emotional strength, cognitive flexibility, and perseverance. It is this intricate tapestry of attributes that empowers individuals to navigate uncertainty with confidence and creativity. This chapter will delve deeply into how these foundational elements of resilience can be cultivated and strengthened to serve as a launchpad for enduring success.

The difference between having a growth mindset and a fixed mindset is crucial in determining how you respond to challenges. Where a fixed mindset sees obstacles as unbeatable and capabilities as unchangeable, a growth mindset perceives challenges as opportunities to learn and develop. Embracing a growth mindset is crucial for building resilience, as it encourages you to view setbacks as stepping stones rather than stumbling blocks. By shifting perspective and valuing effort and persistence, the growth mindset cultivates resilience by nurturing a belief in the potential for growth and evolution. This transformative shift in mentality allows you to engage more deeply in your pursuits, take calculated risks, and stay open to new opportunities.

Embracing resilience as a lifelong skill transforms it from a reactive force into a proactive tool, essential for navigating the ever-evolving challenges of life. Unlike transient skills that may lose relevance, resilience evolves with us, adapting to our changing circumstances and needs. As a lifelong skill, resilience requires continuous nurturing and development, similar to honing any other craft. It involves conscious practice, reflection, and the willingness to embrace discomfort and uncertainty as avenues for development. Whether you're adapting to sweeping career changes, managing personal trials, or pursuing audacious aspirations, resilience ensures that you remain anchored and capable of steering towards your desired outcomes. Reflecting on my own journey, I have discovered that adopting a growth mindset has empowered me to view each challenge as an invaluable lesson rather than an insurmountable barrier. This shift has not only enhanced my resilience but also opened doors to opportunities I might have otherwise overlooked.

By understanding resilience as a dynamic and ongoing journey rather than a destination, we position ourselves to lead lives defined by tenacity and purpose. The first step in this journey is recognizing that resilience is not an inherent trait but a skill that can be learned and refined. As we explore the principles outlined in this chapter, they will be equipped with the tools and frameworks necessary to foster resilience in their own lives. The insights gained will illuminate the power of resilience to propel you forward, allowing you to transcend limitations, build on strengths, and uncover potential that was previously obscured by the shadows of doubt and fear. More than just a mechanism for overcoming obstacles, resilience emerges as a pathway to a more fulfilling and successful life, where aspirations are sustained by an unwavering resolve and the virtues of fortitude, adaptability, and growth are celebrated. As you embark on this journey, remember that resilience is not simply about enduring life's storm but learning to dance in the rain, crafting success from perseverance and vision.

The Foundation of Resilience

The foundation of resilience is an complex totality woven from self-awareness, adaptability, and a purposeful mindset. It starts with self-awareness and emotional regulation, which serve as the cornerstone of resilience. By cultivating a deep understanding of our emotions, thoughts, and behaviours, we become skilled navigators of our internal landscapes. Self-awareness empowers us to identify stress triggers and emotional responses, allowing us to harness them constructively. Emotional regulation further enhances this foundation by equipping us with the ability to manage emotions effectively. This not only shields us from impulsive reactions but also enables us to remain composed in challenging situations. Embracing mindfulness practices, such as meditation or journaling, aids in deepening this self-awareness, leading to a more reflective and adjusted approach to life's trials. In the busy rush of daily life, we rarely pause to think about our position among our many responsibilities and ambitions. This often leads us to follow routines automatically instead of planning a clear path toward our goals.

In tandem with self-awareness, adaptability, optimism, and a positive mindset form another crucial pillar of resilience. The world around us is in constant flux, and the capacity to adapt is essential in thriving amid uncertainty. Adaptability fosters resilience by encouraging flexibility in response to change, reframing setbacks as opportunities for growth, and propelling us toward innovative solutions. An optimistic outlook further propels this adaptability, allowing us to see the potential within challenges. Cultivating a positive mindset is more than superficial positivity; it's about nurturing an authentic belief in one's ability to navigate adversity and emerge stronger. It involves framing difficulties not as insurmountable obstacles, but as chances to learn and evolve. As this mindset takes root, it not only supports our resilience but also colors our perceptions, influencing how we engage with the world.

Purpose, meaning, and desire are the final crucial components underpinning resilience. Resilience gains momentum and direction when it is anchored in a sense of purpose. Understanding what is truly meaningful in our lives provides a beacon during chaotic times. When aligned with our core desires and values, purpose becomes a driving force that fuels persistent determination. It acts as a compass, guiding us through challenges and helping to distinguish between what truly deserves our energy and what does not. This essential motivation is vital, transforming resilience into a proactive force rather than a passive response. By cultivating a strong sense of purpose, we are able to tap into profound reserves of inner strength, enabling us to transcend obstacles with determination and clarity. How often do you pause to reflect on the reasons behind your actions, ensuring that they align with your core values and purpose, guiding you towards fulfilling your true potential?

Together, these elements build an impressive foundation for resilience. As we develop self-awareness, adapt to change with optimism, and align with a sense of purpose, we discover the ability to shape our response to life's diverse challenges. They are not merely isolated practices but interdependent skills that, when nurtured, empower us to master resilience as a strategic and dynamic process. With these insights at our disposal, we transform resilience into a proactive, empowering strategy to navigate life's complexities and achieve a fulfilling, meaningful existence. Through deliberate practice and reflection, we un-cover the potential within ourselves, realizing that resilience is not about surviving against all odds but flourishing in spite of them.

The Growth Mindset vs. Fixed Mindset

In understanding the difference between growth and fixed mindsets, it is essential to recognize how these paradigms shape our approach to challenges and personal development. A growth mindset, a concept popularized by numerous psychologists, is the belief that our abilities and intelligence can be developed through hard work, perseverance, and dedication. It emphasizes the potential for improvement and learning, viewing failure as a stepping stone to greater understanding and skill. Conversely, a fixed mindset is characterized by the belief that abilities and intelligence are static, inherent traits that cannot be changed. This perspective often leads to a fear of failure and an aversion to challenges, as they may expose perceived deficiencies. Adopting a growth mindset significantly enhances resilience, as it encourages adaptability and the capacity to learn from setbacks. Real-life examples abound of individuals who have harnessed a growth mindset to achieve remarkable success. Consider Thomas Edison, whose relentless experimentation and refusal to view failures as the end allowed him to invent the light bulb after countless unsuccessful attempts. Similarly, the evolution of technology giants illustrates how embracing innovation, and learning can lead to extraordinary breakthroughs. They did it, so why couldn't you? With resilience and the power of will, you have the ability to achieve remarkable success and overcome any challenges you face.

Reframing challenges as opportunities for growth is a cornerstone of developing resilience. This mindset shift involves viewing obstacles not as insurmountable barriers, but as valuable learning experiences that contribute to personal and professional development. Reducing the fear of failure by understanding challenges as stepping stones alleviates the anxiety associated with trying new pursuits. Techniques for reframing setbacks include identifying lessons in each failure and recognizing even the smallest of progressions, which build confidence over time. In this way, setbacks are no longer feared, but rather embraced as opportunities to accumulate knowledge and skills that enhance one's journey.

To transition from a fixed to a growth mindset, practical steps are necessary. The first step is self-awareness – recognizing and acknowledging any fixed-mindset beliefs that may be holding you back. This awareness creates room for change and growth. An effective method involves using growth-oriented language. You should start by replacing "I'm not good at this" with "I can improve this skill." Such language not only shifts your perspective but also empowers the pursuit of personal advancement. Additionally, setting small, achievable goals reinforces the concept of incremental growth, allowing you to celebrate each milestone, however minor it may seem, as a testament to improvement and effort. Like small rivers that feed into larger ones, minor actions can lead to significant life changes. Every small step toward growth and self-improvement contributes to a larger journey of success.

The transformation towards a growth mindset is rooted in consistent, deliberate actions and reflections that steer you toward potential untapped in static beliefs. By embracing a growth mindset, challenges become welcomed opportunities to evolve, resilience solidifies into an empowering strategic process, and the path to personal fulfilment becomes navigable with courage and clarity. In fostering this mindset, we discover that resilience is not merely about enduring life's storms, but about thriving amidst them, armed with the knowledge that each experience enriches and propels us forward in our lifelong journey of learning and growth.

Embracing Resilience as a Lifelong Skill

Embracing resilience as a lifelong skill is important for personal growth and success. Recognizing resilience as a continual practice involves defining it as a skill honed over time through consistent effort, learning, and self-reflection. With each experience, resilience strengthens and enhances our ability to adapt to challenges, making us better individuals. Persistent individuals who commit to resilience and personal growth demonstrate how these qualities foster ongoing success. For instance, figures like Nelson Mandela and Malala Yousafzai have shown how resilience, combined with a desire for growth, can overcome immense obstacles and lead to meaningful change, demonstrating that perseverance alongside self-development shapes their journey. Remember, just as Rome wasn't built in a day, achieving lasting growth and resilience requires patience and persistence, so keep pushing forward without giving up.

Viewing setbacks as building blocks for resilience and growth is crucial. Each setback becomes an opportunity to cultivate resilience while improving yourself. Encouraging the perception of difficulties as learning experiences can significantly contribute to your personal development, making you more adaptable and resilient. Practical strategies for processing setbacks constructively include journaling lessons learned, setting personal growth goals, or identifying new skills to develop. Adopting such methods fosters a mindset that transforms challenges into stepping stones for further growth, helping you become more equipped to face future adversities with a growth-oriented attitude. Initially, it might seem difficult to view setbacks in a positive light, as they often appear to slow down our progress. However, upon reflection, these challenges often catalyze personal growth, empowering us to become stronger, more competent versions of ourselves, driven by an inner will to become better in what we do.

Incorporating resilience and personal growth into your daily life involves small, consistent actions that build resilience and a desire for self-improvement. Setting micro-goals offers a powerful means to motivate yourself and track your progress, facilitating consistent growth. Practicing mindfulness encourages present-moment awareness, enhancing emotional resilience by helping you handle stress better. Reflecting on your progress allows you to celebrate improvements and recognize areas requiring further attention. Additionally, cultivating daily habits such as optimism, self-care, gratitude, and learning underpins resilience and ongoing self-improvement. Optimism sustains motivation and a positive outlook, which are instrumental in weathering life's ups and downs. Engaging in self-care routines revitalizes your mind and body, equipping you to react to challenges.

Gratitude is powerful in these practices, shifting focus to positivity and appreciation, which boosts emotional strength and resilience. Lifelong learning encourages adaptability and openness to new perspectives, reinforcing personal growth. By incorporating these habits into daily routines, resilience can be fortified, personal boundaries pushed in the pursuit of self-betterment, with each moment contributing to the lifelong journey. Viewing resilience as part of a lifelong journey is empowering. Committing to adaptability and personal development aspires one to become a better individual continuously. Such a commitment means embracing change and uncertainty with poise, using each experience as a lesson conducive to growth.

This approach transforms life into a rewarding journey, with resilience as your reliable companion. By learning to harness resilience, you gain an increased sense of agency over life, feeling better equipped to turn adversities into lessons learned and personal milestones achieved. Ultimately, this commitment not only guides you toward your highest potential but also empowers you to drive change in your community, inspiring others through your journey of resilience and personal growth. By viewing each challenge as an opportunity to evolve and every success as a validation of your efforts, you can tap into a wellspring of potential, making resilience a lifelong skill that supports your continuous evolution.

3

Building a Clear Vision and Purpose

Having resilience is essential, but without a defined goal, vision, or purpose, its potential remains untapped. It's time to awaken to the importance of establishing a clear direction in life, enabling resilience to steer you towards transformational success. Vision and purpose form the cornerstone of any successful life strategy. By cultivating a clear sense of direction, a greater focus and tenacity are empowered in navigating the complexities of life. In this chapter, the essential practices that allow personal and professional aspirations to be defined and refined are explored, a course for long-term vision is set, and a resilience-based action plan for progress is developed.

To begin, your exploration will guide you through the process of identifying personal and professional goals. This involves deep reflection on not just what drives your ambitions but also understanding the intrinsic values and motivations that underpin these goals. The journey of self-discovery reveals the desires that truly resonate and align with your authentic self. You're here for a reason, and I believe you're ready to make a change or start chasing your dreams, but it's possible that the sparkle has been missing, or you find yourself always giving up. Perhaps you don't yet know where you're going, but trust me, you will find your purpose if you dig deep. Embracing this mindset is crucial, and as you uncover the layers of your ambitions, you'll start to see the path forming ahead of you. Remember, clarity often comes from exploring your passions and values, paving the way for a journey fueled by dedication and insight. Together, we'll embark on this transformative journey, unveiling the unique purpose that will guide every step you take toward your dreams. By setting specific, measurable, achievable, relevant, and time-bound (SMART) goals, you can create a structured pathway towards success, providing clarity and eliminating distractions along the way.

Crafting a long-term vision is the next critical aspect of building a purposeful life. This process is about painting a vivid picture of where you desire to be in the future, blending passion with practicality in a way that both inspires and grounds you. Such a vision instills hope and nurtures the courage to pursue aspirations regardless of obstacles or setbacks. Imagining the future with deliberate intent allows for a realistic yet ambitious blueprint that serves as a guiding star, ensuring every decision and action is attuned to this envisioned outcome. This future-oriented mindset encourages adaptability, fostering a creative resilience that transforms challenges into opportunities. Dreaming big is exciting and opens up many opportunities. It's important to also consider the time and effort needed to achieve these dreams. Building resilience helps you handle challenges and turn them into opportunities for growth. This resilience ensures your dreams are ambitious yet achievable. Let your dreams guide you, but keep them grounded in reality, so each step combines inspiration with strategic action. Developing a resilience-based action plan is crucial for this project. This plan serves as a roadmap outlining the steps needed to move from the present to desired futures. Resilience is key here—it involves viewing unexpected challenges as part of the growth journey, not just obstacles. Embracing resilience means being flexible, persistent, and positive, and incorporating strategies to tackle and overcome challenges into your action plan.

The synergy between a clear vision, well-defined goals, and a resilience-based plan transforms ambitions into achievable realities. This combination integrates intention with action, fostering a proactive approach to life. Aligning purpose with practice not only enhances satisfaction but also builds a legacy of fulfilled potential. Throughout this chapter, insights and strategies will be provided to empower a journey toward personal development. Consider how these elements interconnect to support the resilience needed to navigate life's challenges.

Ultimately, building a clear vision and purpose is about harnessing inner strength and external actions in a harmonious balance that nurtures continuous growth. By focusing on these key components, you can steer through your life with confidence, ensuring that every endeavour draws them closer to fulfilling their truest potential and contributing profoundly to their personal and professional spheres.

Identifying Personal and Professional Goals

Reflecting on the reason you find yourself on this path, it's evident that a desire for growth propels you forward. Whether you're seeking to enhance your current capabilities or aspiring to reach new heights, the journey begins with acknowledging your current status and envisioning where you want to be. The essential step in this process is to clearly identify your personal or professional goals. Establishing these targets not only provides direction but also channels your energy into meaningful pursuits. Embarking on the journey to identify personal and professional goals starts with clarifying your core values and aspirations. These are the guiding principles and dreams that energize and direct your efforts. Take time to reflect and articulate what truly matters to you, shaping a foundation upon which meaningful goals can be constructed. By understanding your core values, you offer yourself a compass that will steer you toward achievements that resonate with your deepest desires. Identifying what success personally means to you clarifies the significance of your goals and imbues them with purpose. This clarity sustains your energy and determination, ensuring that even when the path is challenging, you remain anchored in why your goals matter. Such alignment between goals and values is essential for maintaining motivation, particularly as you navigate through both expected and unforeseen life circumstances.

Remember, you should not hold yourself back; everyone has their personal values and goals, so don't be ashamed of pursuing what truly matters to you. When setting specific, achievable goals, consider utilizing the SMART criteria we presented earlier. Let this serve as a reminder. This framework serves as a robust structure that transforms ambitions into clear, actionable steps. Setting specific goals removes confusion and creates a clear path; having measurable elements helps you track progress and enjoy small successes. Achievable goals ground your journey in realism, encouraging steady progress rather than overwhelming demands. By ensuring that your goals are relevant, you maintain alignment with your core values and current life context, while time-bound aspects inject a sense of urgency and commitment into your endeavours. Breaking down long-term goals into smaller, manageable milestones helps maintain sustained motivation and simplifies the tracking process. Smaller milestones serve as stepping stones on the path to your ultimate destination, making the journey less daunting and more attainable. Prioritization plays a crucial role in this process, focusing your efforts on goals that cater to immediate needs while simultaneously considering their long-term impact to achieve real results.

Creating a roadmap for personal and professional growth helps translate these goals into actions. Start by mapping out the necessary steps to achieve each goal, considering what resources, skills, or actions are required. Implementing mechanisms to track and celebrate your progress reinforces motivation and cultivates a resilient mindset, turning each achievement into a reminder of your capability and commitment. Remember, the journey toward your goals is not static; adopting a flexible approach allows you to adapt to new opportunities or challenges as they arise. Stay open to refining your goals as you grow, ensuring that your roadmap evolves alongside your personal and professional development. This adaptability ensures that your goals remain aligned with your evolving vision and purpose, nurturing continuous growth. By embracing this approach to goal-setting, you empower yourself to create a future tailored to your aspirations, built upon a resilient and purposeful foundation. In doing so, you lay the groundwork for a fulfilling path that not only achieves your personal milestones but also contributes meaningfully to your broader life's journey.

Crafting Your Long-Term Vision

Imagining your ideal future self requires a deep dive into the core aspects of life you wish to achieve. Begin by picturing what a fulfilling personal and professional life looks like for you. Let your imagination explore the multifaceted dimensions of success, happiness, and growth. Identify the values and principles that resonate with you most, allowing them to illuminate your path forward. By articulating a vision that is inspiring and deeply meaningful, you create a powerful source of resilience and motivation, propelling you forward even when faced with challenges. This vision, imbued with purpose, becomes the stepping stone for achieving a life that truly aligns with your unique identity and aspirations. While it's essential to dream big and aim high, remember to stay grounded in reality. Achieving your vision requires patience and persistence, as meaningful accomplishments take time and effort to materialize.

Once this ideal vision is clear, the next strategic move involves dissecting it into significant milestones. These milestones act as markers on your journey, transforming an overwhelming vision into a sequence of attainable and manageable steps. Think of them as signposts guiding you toward your desired destination. Define specific outcomes associated with each milestone, prioritizing those elements that hold the greatest significance for your personal growth and professional development. In doing so, you lay out a roadmap that not only clarifies the path ahead but also helps maintain focus on what truly matters. Tracking your progress becomes a ritual that reinforces commitment, celebrating milestones along the way fortifies resilience, and reminds you of your ever-unfolding potential. Sure, this path may seem daunting, but the key is to start taking those first steps.

I've set a ten-year goal that's driving me toward my ambitions. It's not etched in stone, serving instead as a flexible guideline that keeps my focus intact. With each lesson learned, my path becomes clearer, affirming my commitment to where I aim to go.

Crafting a succinct and powerful vision statement is an integral part of this process. This statement should encapsulate your long-term goals and aspirations, serving as a beacon that guides your everyday decisions. When faced with choices that affect your trajectory, a clear vision statement acts as a filter, ensuring each decision aligns with your overarching goals. It grounds your actions in purpose, offering a strategic compass that keeps you true to your path. Revisit and refine your vision periodically to account for growth and changes in perspective. This reflective process ensures that your vision continues to evolve, supporting resilience and adaptability in an ever-changing world. Embrace this as an opportunity to recalibrate and strengthen your dedication to both your vision and the journey itself. Every now and then, I go back to the drawing board and check if my vision is still valid; thus far, it has been. I consistently remind myself of what should be done and strive to stay on track. When challenges arise, resilience fuels my perseverance, and I find strength in the vision I've crafted. This ongoing process assures me that I am aligned with the path I have chosen, reinforcing my commitment to see it through.

Thus, the creation of a long-term vision is not a one-time task but an ongoing commitment to self-discovery, resilience, and strategic personal development. As you imagine your future self and define the stepping stones to get there, infuse your vision with authenticity by aligning it with your deepest values and aspirations. This connection empowers you to pursue a future built on passion and purpose, laying a robust foundation that supports continuous growth. By maintaining focus on your long-term vision, you transform challenges into opportunities and pursue a life that not only meets your personal milestones but also contributes meaningfully to the broader tapestry of your life's journey.

Creating a Resilience-Based Action Plan

To avoid stagnation on your journey towards your vision, create a strategic, resilience-driven action plan. Without this, progress can seem elusive. Identify key objectives and break them into manageable tasks. Anticipate obstacles and plan proactive solutions to build resilience. This empowers you to move forward confidently and adapt to challenges. A dynamic plan acts as your compass, guiding you steadily towards your goals. Seize the moment – craft your action plan and move forward with determination and foresight. Creating a resilience-based action plan is an empowering way to bridge the gap between where you are and where you aspire to be. The first step in this pursuit is setting realistic, actionable goals that reinforce resilience by forming a clear connection to your long-term vision. This process begins with understanding that each goal should feel purposeful, acting as a stepping stone toward achieving your broader aspirations. To enhance resilience, break down large, daunting goals into smaller, manageable steps as mentioned before. This approach not only makes your objectives feel more attainable but also provides opportunities to build resilience through the momentum of steady progress. If your long-term vision involves career advancement, a practical, manageable goal could be to enhance a specific skill set or to commit 30 minutes daily to work toward your primary objective. This kind of incremental progress solidifies your path, ensuring that each small victory contributes to your larger vision. So please stop scrolling and wasting your time. Start doing something meaningful. That is what I have done, and it has worked for me – so why not for you?

A key element of this plan is building accountability and sup-port systems, as these structures uphold resilience during your journey. Accountability can take different forms, from setting deadlines and tracking progress to celebrating each milestone, no matter how small. Acknowledge the importance of creating a supportive network that includes mentors or accountability partners who can offer guidance, feedback, and encouragement. Whether you choose to answer to yourself or to someone else, the key is that this commitment propels you toward achieving your goals. It's essential that this accountability serves as a driving force in your journey. Constructive feedback is also invaluable, as it does not only boost resilience but also refines your action plan, aligning it more closely with your goals. For example, maintaining a journal or using a digital app to document daily actions can aid in tracking your progress. Concurrently, set up a weekly check-in with a friend pursuing similar goals to share successes and challenges, providing mutual motivation and insights. Even if it's just a baby step, sharing your adventures with your spouse can work wonders. They might roll their eyes at first, but once they see your progress, their pride and support can be the wind beneath your wings—or at least a cheerful tailwind.

In addition to realistic goals and supportive networks, em-bedding daily habits and routines is crucial in resilience perspective. Such habits serve as daily anchors that keep you aligned with your vision and reinforce adaptability. Start by incorporating resilience-boosting practices, like mindfulness or regular exercise, that support overall focus and mental adaptability. Establish a routine where each day begins with a brief review of primary goals and a list of three focused actions that propel you forward. It might seem counterintuitive at first. But many successful individuals use these practices to stay focused and motivated. Perhaps it's worth considering how these habits could enhance your own routine. These small, daily rituals reinforce the connection to your larger vision, enhancing your resilience to external changes. Equally important is the need to periodically review and adjust these habits to ensure their continued relevance and effectiveness in supporting your long-term aims. Monthly reflections can be an excellent opportunity to adapt or refine routines that no longer serve their purpose, allowing you to stay flexible yet firmly anchored in your aspirations.

By tightly interweaving these elements – setting realistic, incremental goals, leveraging accountability and support, and solidifying daily habits – your resilience-based action plan becomes a powerful tool. It guides you steadily toward achieving your long-term vision, with the flexibility to adapt to life's inevitable changes without losing motivation or direction. As each goal is achieved, new ones will naturally emerge, per-petuating a cycle of continuous growth and resilience, always aligned with your persona aspirations. This empowers you to navigate challenges confidently, transforming obstacles into opportunities for development and ensuring that each step of your journey contributes meaningfully to the broader tapestry of your life's vision.

4

Developing Mental Toughness for Everyday Challenges

The more often you show up to fight for your goals, the faster you proceed. Every day is not going to be easy, but it will get easier as you elevate your mental toughness. This process is similar to building a muscle; it requires consistent effort and perseverance. So, try to show up every day and become better, little by little. As the complexities of modern life are navigated, mental toughness is developed as an essential skill, enabling everyday challenges to be tackled with confidence and grace. In this chapter, the fundamental aspects of building mental toughness are explored with a comprehensive roadmap offered that highlights the significant roles of discipline, overcoming self-doubt and negative self-talk, and managing stress and adversity effectively. Discipline, seen as a key part of resilience, will be examined not just as following rules but as a powerful tool that turns goals into actions. It acts as a foundation for handling life's challenges, offering the structure and consistency needed to overcome setbacks. With discipline, you can develop a mindset that sees challenges as chances to grow, building a strong framework that supports determination and focus.

Building on the foundation of discipline, we will address the critical task of overcoming self-doubt and negative self-talk, which can undermine self-efficacy and threaten to derail personal progress. These pervasive internal monologues are often acted upon as formidable barriers, with potential stifled and the resolve needed to pursue goals diminished. By identifying and confronting these self-imposed limitations, strategies for reframing thoughts are learned, transforming negativity into positive affirmations and self-belief. Way too often we think that we are not good enough and that we are not worth it. Even though these thoughts may arise, it is crucial to recognize that with will and resilience, improvement is always within reach. The first step is understanding that no matter your current position, there is always the possibility to elevate yourself. This shift in mindset clears the path toward personal achievement and strengthens the mental fortitude required to face life's inevitable challenges. With practice and persistence, more resilient attitudes develop, as the harms of self-doubt are countered by new strength and positivity.

Finally, we will explore effective ways to handle stress and adversity, two common challenges that test our mental strength. Learning how to anticipate, cope with, and adjust to these challenges is crucial for building resilience. This section equips you with tools to thoughtfully handle stress, such as mindfulness practices, prioritization techniques, and adaptive coping mechanisms. By managing stress effectively, you protect mental health, mitigate negative impacts, and maintain a proactive approach in the face of adversity. Together, these insights offer a comprehensive strategy for personal empowerment.

hey reveal a path where discipline, self-awareness, and stress management converge to foster a resilient and flourishing life. As you begin this journey through the chapter, you will gain valuable insights and practical methods to meet everyday challenges with a bold, strategic, and resilient mindset. By integrating these elements into daily life, obstacles can become stepping stones, continuously driving growth and mental strength in the ever-changing landscape of life's demands.

The Role of Discipline in Building Resilience

Have you ever given deep thought to how much discipline truly shapes your responses to life's challenges? Consider the pivotal role it plays in overcoming obstacles and achieving goals. Reflecting on its importance, are you consciously and strategically channelling your discipline to empower your personal growth, enhance your resilience, and manage life's complexities more effectively? We must acknowledge that in the journey of developing mental toughness, discipline plays a crucial role in building resilience, serving as the backbone that supports our ability to navigate life's challenges with strength and determination. Establishing consistent habits is fundamental to this process, as small, daily actions accumulate over time to create a solid foundation for resilience. In moments of reflection, we all sometimes question what we've truly achieved by the end of the day. The answer can be unsettling, often due to a lack of discipline or laziness. This feeling occurs because the routine meant to propel us forward may not be solidly in place. However, recognizing these lapses is the first step towards change. By incorporating routines that offer stability and focus, you can fortify your mental resilience progressively. Take, for instance, the simple act of dedicating five minutes in the morning to a planning session. Or imagine waking up just a bit earlier to devote 30 minutes to studying, writing, or advancing a project you've been passionate about. This use of time can fuel progress and give you a sense of accomplishment early in the day. By tackling critical tasks first thing in the morning, you set a positive tone that helps you to face the rest of the day's challenges with clarity and determination. This habit, replacing the usual phone-checking ritual, is much more productive and better for your mental health. Consistent, disciplined actions build momentum, ultimately making it easier to sustain resilience amid life's inevitable challenges.

Moreover, staying committed despite distractions and challenges is a testament to the power of discipline in enhancing resilience. Life is full of tempting distractions and unexpected setbacks that can derail your progress. This is where discipline becomes crucial. By staying focused on your long-term goals, you can resist the urge for immediate gratification that doesn't align with your objectives. Set limits on activities that consume your time unproductively, like unchecked social media use. For example, by setting a timer to limit your social media scrolling, you can then use that time to learn a new skill or work on a personal project. This disciplined approach builds resilience. By committing to self-accountability, you ensure progress continues even without external motivation, empowering you to stay on track with your journey. I admit that sometimes it is not easy to start your daily study or writing session, especially with hectic projects and temptations are competing for your attention. However, once you begin, the momentum builds, and it becomes significantly easier to continue. Reminding yourself of your goals and reflecting on how each step brings you closer to achieving them can transform challenges into milestones on your journey forward.

Practicing self-control emerges as another vital component of discipline in handling stress and adversity. In turbulent situations, the ability to regulate emotions becomes important for maintaining resilience. Discipline cultivates self-control, enabling you to respond with composure rather than reacting impulsively. Techniques such as pausing before acting can significantly enhance resilience by facilitating calm and deliberate responses. Setting personal boundaries further aids in aligning actions with values and goals, thereby mitigating stress and honing focus. Consider a scenario where facing a frustrating task can trigger a reactive response. By encouraging a pause and regroup instead of an immediate reaction, it empowers an approach to challenges with a calm and resilient mindset. During stressful times, pause and ask yourself, "Is this moving me forward?" Reflect on why you feel stressed, as this can reveal underlying issues. By addressing these questions, you'll often find empowering solutions that reduce stress and strengthen your ability to overcome challenges. These disciplined practices form the bedrock upon which resilience is built, contributing to a life where stress is managed thoughtfully, and challenges are met with a fortified sense of purpose.

Together, these insights illuminate the role of discipline in developing resilience. Whether through establishing consistent habits, staying committed in the face of distractions, or practicing self-control, each aspect underscores how discipline supports resilience. By integrating these principles into daily life, one is equipped to transform obstacles into opportunities for growth, creating a resilient mindset capable of thriving in the dynamic landscape of everyday demands. Embracing the empowering influence of discipline enables a proactive approach to life's challenges, fostering a strong, strategic foundation upon which personal empowerment is continuously constructed.

Overcoming Self-Doubt and Negative Self-Talk

Think about how often you engage in self-reflection and the nature of the dialogue you have with yourself. Is it more positive or negative? Unfortunately, negative self-talk often takes over, as if it's ingrained in us. However, it is important to remember that this outcome is not inevitable and can be influenced by various factors. While external influences may attempt to sow seeds of doubt, fostering a deliberate, positive internal dialogue is important for self-empowerment and resilience. Recognizing and challenging limiting beliefs is the first step in overcoming self-doubt and negative self-talk, which can be significant barriers to developing resilience. Many of us experience self-doubt when faced with new challenges or when stepping out of their comfort zone. It often arises from deeply ingrained, limiting beliefs that can cloud one's judgment and undermine confidence. To combat this, we should start by identifying situations or thoughts that trigger these beliefs. This self-awareness is the first step toward breaking detrimental patterns. Once aware, it becomes easier to question the validity of these beliefs: are they based on fact or simply on fear? For instance, if you feel, "I'm not skilled enough for this project," challenge this belief by evaluating the evidence supporting it—often, there isn't any. Instead, reframe it with empowering thoughts, such as, "This project will help me develop the skills I need." This subtle yet profound shift in perspective transforms challenges into opportunities for growth, thereby strengthening your resilience.

In addition to reframing limiting beliefs, using positive affirmations is an effective strategy to build confidence and combat self-doubt. Positive affirmations are deliberate statements that promote self-belief and optimism, counteracting the negativity of self-doubt. We should be encouraged to craft affirmations that resonate personally, using language that is genuine and inspiring. The daily practice of repeating these affirmations can significantly bolster resilience, particularly during moments of uncertainty. For instance, someone feeling insecure in a new job might use affirmations like, "I am learning and growing every day," which emphasize the value of progress over perfection.

Our mindset is shaped by the stories we tell ourselves, and although it might seem simple, it takes time to master. Positivity is a guiding force, similar to how children thrive with positive affirmations. These affirmations help them become brave, capable, and confident in their abilities. As we grow older, environmental factors and negative self-talk can weaken this confidence. To regain the self-assurance we had as children, we need to consciously reverse this trend. Using affirmations like "I am capable" and "I can succeed," and recognizing our achievements, helps us rediscover the pride and potential we often overlook. This approach not only restores our childhood confidence but also empowers us to achieve new levels in our personal and professional lives. By consistently reinforcing positive affirmations, you have the power to gradually build a positive mindset, celebrate small achievements, and strengthen your belief in your own capabilities.

Another integral aspect of overcoming self-doubt is cultivating a supportive inner dialogue, as mentioned in the previous paragraph. How individuals speak to themselves during challenging times can greatly influence their resilience and overall mental well-being. Encouraging oneself with phrases such as "I can handle this" helps to motivate and instil confidence, even in demanding situations. It's beneficial to treat yourself with the same kindness and empathy you would offer a friend. This involves reframing self-criticism into constructive feedback, which is conducive to learning and self-improvement. For example, if someone perceives a failed task as a personal shortcoming, they should consciously transition from thinking, "I always mess things up" to "What can I learn from this experience?" This practice not only nurtures a resilient mindset but also transforms setbacks into insightful lessons. Sometimes, using anger as a spark for change can be effective. Instead of letting it weigh you down, try flipping that negative energy into positive fuel. Aim to transform defeatist thoughts into empowering ones. When channelled wisely, anger sometimes becomes a tool for growth, helping you climb out of the remorse hole. Get fired up and let it occasionally work in your favor!

But the main message here is that by promoting a nurturing and compassionate inner voice, we can build a foundation of resilience that supports us in facing everyday challenges with confidence and fortitude. Through these interconnected strategies of addressing limiting beliefs, practicing positive affirmations, and fostering a supportive inner dialogue, we can develop a robust inner strength. This empowers navigating life's challenges strategically, viewing each hurdle as an opportunity to grow and enhance mental toughness for the future.

Managing Stress and Adversity Effectively

Stress is an inevitable component of life, manifesting in both negative and positive forms. Negative stress, commonly known as distress, arises when challenges overwhelm our capacity to cope, leading to feelings of anxiety, depression, and decreased performance. This type of stress can be detrimental, undermining mental health and overall well-being. Conversely, positive stress, or eustress, acts as a motivating force, encouraging growth and peak performance. It is the exciting feeling we experience when tackling a challenging project or trying something new. Distinguishing between these types of stress is crucial for understanding how to harness positive stress as a powerful catalyst for personal and professional development, while managing negative stress with effective coping mechanisms. In developing mental toughness for everyday challenges, managing stress and adversity effectively is paramount. One of the key strategies in this realm is practicing mindfulness. Mindfulness allows you to stay grounded by focusing on the present, thereby reducing the inclination to dwell on past difficulties or worry about future uncertainties. By centering your attention on the here and now, mindfulness can significantly decrease emotional reactivity, enabling you to respond to stressors with calmness and clarity. Cultivate a keen awareness of your goals and the positive aspects of your life, acknowledging the strengths you possess. Focus your energy on what you can control, and let go of what lies beyond your influence, thereby channelling your efforts into effective change and personal empowerment. Integrating mindfulness into your routine can be accomplished through simple daily exercises such as brief meditations or deep breathing. For instance, when feeling overwhelmed at work, taking a moment to pause and engage in five slow, deep breaths can reset your mind, enhance focus, and alleviate stress. These practices create a calm atmosphere, helping you face challenges with a clear and composed mindset.

Moreover, reframing adversity as a learning opportunity is a transformative approach. Each setback should be seen not as a source of loss but as a chance to learn, adapt, and grow. This shift in perspective is crucial for building resilience and mental toughness. Rather than getting stuck in frustration or worry, try focusing on solving the problem by taking actionable steps. For example, if you miss an important deadline, rather than fixating on the setback, consider it as an opportunity to refine planning or improve time management strategies to prevent such occurrences in the future. Use the time to reflect on what led to this situation and how you can avoid it in the future, considering whether it was due to a lack of resilience, willpower, or experience. Once you understand the reasons behind it, focus on strengthening these areas for personal growth. This mindset encourages continuous development, turning obstacles into stepping stones for personal growth. By focusing on solutions, you enhance your ability to navigate challenges more effectively, resulting in a cumulative strengthening of mental resilience.

Another vital component of managing stress involves setting healthy boundaries. Establishing boundaries is fundamental to conserving energy for tasks and priorities that truly matter, thereby effectively managing stress. It's essential to recognize situations where it's beneficial to say no, as overcommitting can often lead to burnout and heightened stress levels. Even though you consider yourself a superhuman, you must realize there is a limit you cannot exceed; otherwise, things can swiftly become chaotic. Willpower and resilience must be accompanied by common sense and reasonable thinking to navigate life's complexities effectively. Embracing my own limitations has been a big help on the journey. Realizing I'm not immortal, I still ambitiously challenge myself beyond perceived limits. This pushes me to work harder and be more productive, all while aiming for greatness with a sense of balance. By juggling reality with the allure of endless potential, I've sharpened my resilience and personal growth. This mindset fuels my ambitions, keeps my feet on the ground, and turns experiences into growth opportunities—an immortal pursuit of excellence with a dash of common sense. However, if you find yourself overwhelmed with tasks, it might be advantageous to set a boundary that stops you from working beyond a certain hour each evening. This not only conserves energy but also allocates time for recharging activities such as reading, engaging in hobbies, or spending quality time with loved ones. Regular breaks or self-care routines are indispensable in promoting relaxation and well-being, ultimately supporting long-term resilience. By prioritizing self-care and maintaining these boundaries, you fortify your capacity to handle stressors with agility and strength.

In conclusion, these strategies – practicing mindfulness, reframing adversity as a learning opportunity, and setting healthy boundaries—not only aid in addressing immediate stressors but also lay the groundwork for sustained mental toughness. By incorporating mindfulness, you achieve a balanced perspective, reframing adversity fosters a resilient growth mindset, and strategic boundaries ensure sustained energy for the challenges ahead. Each of these elements plays an integral role in developing the robust mental framework needed to face life's everyday challenges with confidence and strength.

5

Breaking Free from Mental and Physical Barriers

Mental and physical barriers are obstacles that hinder personal progress and achievement. Mental barriers often stem from self-doubt, fear, or limiting beliefs that restrict one's potential. On the other hand, physical barriers can include health limitations or environmental factors that prevent individuals from reaching their goals. In our journey towards personal growth and achievement, we often encounter both mental and physical barriers that hinder our progress. Breaking free from these limitations is essential to unlock our full potential and embrace a life of empowerment and success. In this chapter we explore this transformative process, guiding you through the identification and understanding of these limiting barriers, strategies to break through them, and the creation of new, empowering habits to support your path forward.

The first step in overcoming mental and physical barriers lies in identifying and understanding them. Frequently, these barriers manifest in the form of self-doubt, fear, or misconceptions about our abilities and potential. They can be deeply ingrained in our mindset or influenced by external factors such as societal expectations and past experiences. We are the sum of our experiences, our surroundings, and the people around us. Understanding this interconnectedness allows us to recognize the impact of our environment and relationships on our mindset and actions. By acknowledging and examining these barriers, we can gain insight into their origins and impact on our lives. Understanding these obstacles is a powerful act of self-awareness that sets the stage for transformative change.

Once you have identified the barriers holding you back, the next critical phase involves developing effective strategies for breaking through them. It's important to adopt a systematic approach that addresses both mental and physical aspects, empowering you to dismantle these limitations with precision and confidence. Techniques such as cognitive restructuring, visualization, and setting incremental goals can be instrumental in altering your mindset, allowing you to see obstacles as surmountable challenges rather than insurmountable walls. Additionally, incorporating physical actions—such as regular exercise and focused breathing exercises – can enhance your overall well-being, providing the energy and resilience needed to push past constraints. Strategic planning, persistence, and a willingness to adapt are essential tools in this phase, equipping you with the capacity to transform barriers into stepping stones for success.

The culmination of understanding and overcoming barriers leads to the creation of new, empowering habits. Habits are powerful because they shape our daily actions and, ultimately, the trajectory of our lives. By establishing routines that align with your goals and values, you can reinforce positive changes and maintain momentum on your journey. This is where intentionality plays a significant role. Establishing habits that support your personal and professional aspirations ensures that your actions consistently contribute to your growth rather than detract from it. For example, adopting a routine that priori-tizes self-care and time for reflection can fortify your resolve and enhance mental clarity, while incorporating learning and skill-building activities can propel you towards achieving your objectives. New habits become the bedrock upon which you can build sustained success, enabling you to flourish beyond any barriers you previously encountered.

As we explore these key points further in the subsequent sections of this chapter, you will be equipped with practical insights and actionable insights to navigate this transformative process. Identifying and understanding your barriers is the foundation; breaking through them is the breakthrough, and building new, empowering habits is the assurance of enduring progress. We cannot do it for you, but by engaging with this chapter, you embark on a journey to free yourself from limiting beliefs and physical constraints. This paves the way towards a life unbounded by limitations and enriched with potential. With determination and insight, you have the power to break free and realize the profound possibilities that lie ahead.

Identifying and Understanding Limiting Barriers

It's hard to start a fight if you don't know who you are fighting with, so start by defining your opponent. Identifying and understanding limiting barriers is a crucial step in the journey of breaking free from mental and physical constraints. Both internal and external barriers can significantly impact persc~ʌl growth and recognizing them is the first move towards overcoming them. Internal barriers often manifest as negative beliefs we harbor about ourselves, such as thoughts like "I'm not capable" or "I don't deserve success." These are not merely thoughts but self-imposed limitations that arise from past experiences, self-comparisons, or fears of failure. By recognizing the origins of these beliefs, we gain the power to transform them. If you consistently tell yourself, "I'm not good with technology," this belief can stifle potential. Reframing it to, "I'm open to learning new tech skills" shifts you from a fixed mindset to one that is growth-oriented and fosters capabilities hitherto unexplored. Remember that it's too easy to claim you're not good at something and leave it at that, as it excuses you from taking action. It's time to awaken your potential and harness the resilience within you to push past these self-imposed limitations.

Furthermore, external barriers, such as environmental factors or lack of resources, can be just as limiting as internal ones. It's essential to evaluate the conditions that restrict your progress, whether they are financial constraints, unsupportive environments, or physical hindrances. Once these are identified, categorize them into those you can control and those that are beyond your reach. This distinction is essential to developing adaptive strategies that either mitigate the impact of these barriers or navigate around them. Choosing your battles strategically is crucial; focus on what you can control and wisely let go of what you cannot change. Attempting to tackle everything simultaneously can lead to burnout, stalling your development process. Employing common sense and a well-defined strategy ensures sustained progress and empowers transformative growth. Begin by concentrating on the single most important task. For instance, if time constraints pose a significant challenge, reorganizing your priorities might be necessary. Creating dedicated blocks of time for significant goals or delegating less critical tasks can turn a seemingly insurmountable barrier into a manageable one. I personally believe that incremental steps and daily dedication guide me in the right direction, especially when time is my greatest constraint. Everyone seems to want a piece of it, which is why I guard it like my most valuable asset, carefully structuring my schedule to focus on what truly matters. Often, this means dedicating early mornings and late evenings to my pursuits, but that's where resilience becomes my ally. Consistent and strategic time management leads to empowerment and ensures that progress is both achievable and sustainable.

The patterns of behaviour we exhibit also contribute to re-inforcing barriers, which often leads to perpetuated cycles of self-sabotage. Behaviours like procrastination, avoidance of challenges, or perfectionism can all fortify the barriers around us. Delving into the root causes of these behaviours, whether they stem from ingrained fear, self-doubt, or an overwhelming desire for control, is paramount. Such reflection can open the door to replacing detrimental habits with positive, growth-oriented ones. Take procrastination, for example. Instituting small, actionable changes such as the "5-minute rule" can significantly reduce the tendency to avoid tasks. By committing to engage with a task for just five minutes, you make the first move toward reducing inertia and fostering progress, gradually eroding the procrastination barrier. Embracing complexity can feel daunting at first, but once you realize there's no single right answer, it really frees up your creativity. With this in mind, I dive into exploration, trusting that clarity will come through action.

ﾞﾟong the way, willpower and resilience are my trusty sidekicks, helping me carve out a path where none seemed possible before.

By integrating an awareness of these internal, external, and behavioural barriers, and by role-modelling techniques to navigate and reshape them, you empower yourself to rise above and transform limitations into stepping stones for growth. Applying these insights not only strengthens your resilience but also sets the stage for having more control in your own life. By taking strategic actions and thoughtfully addressing personal challenges, you can unlock your full potential and create a rewarding path free from fear and self-imposed limits. Embracing the courage to understand and overcome these barriers aligns your journey with a more enriching story, fostering an environment that nurtures both current abilities and future opportunities.

Strategies for Breaking Through Barriers

To break through both mental and physical barriers, building an unbreakable action plan requires immense determination. This process is not just about reducing the anxiety that comes with large goals, but about embracing each step as a challenge to be tackled with unwavering resolve. By dissecting monumental tasks into smaller, more manageable steps, we commit to each action with the dedication needed to forge ahead. Reaching each milestone serves as a testament to our strength and persistence, reinforcing our will to continue even when difficulties arise. Take the example of learning a new skill that, at first glance, may seem overwhelming. By dedicating just 15 minutes each day, you are effectively building a routine that promises incremental growth. Each of these sessions strengthens not only your skill but your willpower, steadily constructing a resilience that arms you for the greater challenges ahead. I used this method to write this book, for instance. When faced with the challenge of finding time amidst a busy schedule, I made a conscious decision to carve out dedicated moments and break the task into small, daily actions. Every day, I committed to writing a bit more, and gradually, the book started taking shape. It wasn't about making drastic changes or finding a large chunk of free time; it was about staying consistent and viewing each writing session as a crucial piece of the bigger puzzle. Little by little, this approach pushed the project forward and eventually brought it to completion. It's a testament to the power of strategic, incremental efforts.

Visualization is another powerful strategy that taps into our inner strength and desire for change. By vividly imagining the experience of overcoming your barriers, you create a pool of motivation that propels you forward. Visualization isn't just about the result. It spans the journey, fostering a mindset prepared for the inevitable obstacles. By picturing the effort and commitment needed, you mentally ready yourself for the hard work that accompanies real progress. Reinforce this process by making visualization a daily practice, using the emotions of achievement as fuel. Imagine taking on a challenging project. By spending a few minutes each day picturing yourself overcoming obstacles with determination, you can build confidence and visualize the satisfaction of future success. I personally use visualization as a cornerstone of my goal orientation, and it's a game-changer. By clearly picturing where I want to be, I gain the clarity needed to differentiate between what's essential and what's not. It's like having a mental map that guides my decisions and prioritizes my actions. When I visualize my goals, the path forward becomes more evident, allowing me to focus on the steps that truly matter and disregard distractions that don't serve my purpose. If I can do it, so can you, so let's dive into the world of visualization together.

Finally, incorporate creating accountability systems to drive relentless effort. The journey to overcoming obstacles is seldom a solitary one. Surrounding yourself with individuals who share your determination not only creates a supportive environment but also champions the perseverance and hard work needed. Remember, you are the average of the people that surround you, so choose wisely to ensure they uplift and inspire your journey towards success. Employ regular progress checks as a tool to maintain motivation and confront any setbacks. Acknowledge each achieved milestone as evidence of your resilience and the formidable strength it took to break through limitations. For instance, aligning yourself with a partner who shares your goals can be instrumental. Together, you can commit to mutual support, using each other's progress as encouragement. Celebrate these moments as landmarks of resilience that reinforce the desire to continue thriving against challenges. Collectively, these strategies lay the groundwork for a renewed, empowering journey towards meeting and surpassing personal limitations with strategic insight and powerful resolve.

Building New, Empowering Habits

In the journey of breaking free from mental and physical barriers, building new, empowering habits plays a pivotal role. In the previous chapters, we've touched on creating new habits, but now it's time to delve deeper and really understand how to make these changes last and transform your habits. The development of these habits is not only about change but about creating a resilient mindset that propels you forward. One effective approach is starting small to build consistency and willpower. Fostering resilience, especially in a business context, begins with manageable steps that are challenging enough to require effort yet simple enough to be consistently integrated into daily routines. Remember, pushing your boundaries is essential for growth, and resilience is the key to staying focused and ahead in this journey. Small actions matter and these small, repeated actions form the backbone of a resilient mindset and gradually build confidence, setting a solid groundwork for more ambitious goals. For instance, if enhancing your business acumen is the goal, begin by dedicating just 10 minutes each day to read industry news or a business book. This small commitment not only strengthens willpower but also builds a foundational knowledge that keeps you informed and prepares you to weather changes and challenges in the industry. Ultimately, the journey of building new habits and achieving your goals arises on the simple principle: it's all about showing up every day.

Furthermore, it is important to reflect on and replace limiting habits with empowering alternatives. Often, existing habits may subtly reinforce limitations by consuming valuable time and energy on distractions or non-productive tasks, such as constantly checking emails or social media. In today's busy world, our ability to focus has diminished as our minds constantly drift due to endless distractions. This tendency to escape mundane tasks slows down our progress significantly. Multitasking, often seen as a skill, isn't the solution. It divides attention and hinders efficiency. Instead, cultivate resilience to get rid of the distractions, dedicating your attention to the goals you're determined to achieve. By consciously choosing to replace these bad habits with actions that directly contribute to your strategic goals, you build resilience with each deliberate decision to focus on impactful activities. For instance, replacing time spent on emails with 15 minutes of strategic planning for a new project aligns your daily actions with long-term goals. This choice strengthens your resilience and willpower by prioritizing growth over distraction.

Additionally, using accountability to strengthen commitment to change is paramount. Personal accountability systems, such as tracking goals or regular self-check-ins, are instrumental in maintaining focus and reinforcing the will to make lasting changes. These systems should align specific checkpoints directly with ultimate goals, ensuring every step taken brings you closer to achieving what you truly desire. But remember, it's crucial to keep things realistic and avoid becoming overly obsessed about it all. A simple conversation with yourself can work wonders and that's something I'm constantly striving to improve daily. Often, just pausing to reflect is sufficient to realign my actions with my priorities. It helps me decide what to focus on now, while trusting that the right time for other tasks will come later. Over time, the dedication starts to show through in the progress you make. By celebrating each milestone reached, you recognize the effort and persistence it took, acknowledging this as evidence of growth and resilience. If your objective is to master a new skill, create a milestone chart highlighting key accomplishments, such as completing courses or mastering new tools. Marking off each milestone not only demonstrates progress but fortifies your willpower, strengthening commitment to continuous personal development. I know it feels tedious to maintain these kinds of systems, but have you really implemented them consistently? If not, that might be the very reason you're seeking a new approach to managing your personal growth and honing your skills. Embracing and committing to these strategies can empower you to transform your intentions into real results, guiding you toward the success you are chasing.

Incorporating these key strategies – starting small, replacing limiting behaviours with empowering habits, and leveraging accountability – lays the foundation for enduring personal growth. This transformative approach supports not only the development of individual resilience and willpower but cultivates a strong, unwavering commitment to embracing change. By integrating these empowering habits into your daily life, you forge a pathway to not only overcoming barriers but thriving amidst them, steadily advancing toward your personal and professional aspirations. It is the cumulative strength of such empowered habits that ultimately drives meaningful and lasting transformation, ensuring you remain resolute and undeterred in the pursuit of your goals. This journey, grounded in strategic planning and informed actions, frees you from limitations and highlights the way to achieving remarkable success.

6

Building Emotional Resilience for Lasting Change

E motional resilience is the ability to adapt to and recover from life's adversities while maintaining a balanced outlook. It equips individuals with the tools to manage stress, maintain optimism, and overcome obstacles without dwelling in defeat. This steadfast trait not only assists in understanding challenges but also opens the door to personal growth and transformation. Building emotional resilience is an essential aspect of achieving lasting change in both personal and professional realms. This chapter aims to provide you with the tools and insights necessary to foster resilience, equipping you to handle life's challenges with grace and determination. Understanding emotional triggers and responses is the first step in this transformative journey. It involves gaining awareness of what emotions are being triggered by various situations and how these sensations influence our behaviours and decisions. By identifying these responses, you gain clarity and control over your emotions, paving the way for more calculated and rational responses. This process not only allows you to navigate challenging situations but also minimizes impulsive reactions and stress.

In tandem with understanding emotional triggers, strengthening emotional intelligence is one important skill. Emotional intelligence involves the ability to recognize, understand, and manage both your emotions and the emotions of others. It forms the bedrock of effective interpersonal communication and relationship-building. By honing this skill, you become skilled at assessing emotional cues and responding with empathy and sensitivity. Enhanced emotional intelligence empowers you to navigate the emotional undercurrents in both your life and work environments, creating healthier interactions and more productive collaborations. As you increase your emotional intelligence, you create an environment where constructive feedback and understanding flourish, essential components for ongoing personal development and adaptability.

The cornerstone of building emotional resilience, however, lies in cultivating a positive, resilient mindset. A positive mindset encourages optimism and fosters a proactive, solution-focused approach in your activities. It redirects focus from challenges to opportunities, turning setbacks into valuable learning experiences. By fostering resilience through positivity, you improve your ability to recover from setbacks and stay motivated despite challenges. A resilient mindset, marked by flexibility and openness to change, boosts your capacity to adapt to new situations and helps you become more resourceful and self-reliant.

Together, these components form an interconnected network that supports your emotional fortitude in achieving lasting change. As you delve deeper into each of these areas, you will uncover strategies to effectively manage your emotional landscape, build stronger relationships, and foster a mindset that is resistant to external pressures yet responsive to new possibilities. Building emotional resilience not only enriches your personal growth but propels you toward accomplishing your long-term goals with heightened confidence and poise. Embrace this journey as a powerful step to help you withstand life's challenges and emerge stronger and more confident. By understanding and applying these principles, you are not only strengthening your emotional defences but also creating a story of resilience that inspires others, spreading positive change beyond your personal sphere. Building a strong base of emotional resilience positions you to not just survive but thrive, shaping a future marked by adaptability, insight, and overcoming adversity. This dedication to emotional resilience is essential for achieving meaningful and lasting success in your pursuit of change.

Understanding Emotional Triggers and Responses

Understanding and managing emotional triggers is a transformative skill essential to building lasting emotional resilience. The first step in this journey is identifying common triggers that may hinder your progress. These triggers often manifest in response to specific situations such as criticism, unexpected challenges, or high-pressure scenarios, which can stir up emotional responses that hold you back. I am convinced that quite a few of us act differently under high pressure. In these moments, it's tougher to grasp how others feel, and our communication style shifts – often becoming sudden and, sometimes, unintentionally hurtful. This approach rarely helps in reaching our shared objectives. That's when it's crucial to pause and reflect on your actions, your behaviour, and your communication style. After all, it's about being resilient. Recognizing triggers requires a keen awareness of the internal beliefs underpinning them, like fear of failure or perfectionism, which intensify emotions when outcomes deviate from expectations. For instance, if you routinely feel defensive when receiving constructive feedback, this could be a sign that your internal narrative equates feedback with personal inadequacy rather than a chance for professional growth. By reinterpreting feedback as an opportunity to learn, you can transform this trigger into a stepping stone towards resilience.

The impact of emotional responses on your path to success is profound. Reactions such as avoidance, defensiveness, or self-doubt can entrench unproductive patterns, limiting your potential for growth and obscuring clear judgment. These unchecked reactions often lead to impulsive decisions or the abandonment of goals in moments of discouragement. So don't hide in your shell after criticism; rise above it with the courage to learn and evolve, empowering every experience. Hence, it is imperative to transition from reactive to proactive responses. This shift can enable you to tackle challenges with resilience, even when faced with unexpected setbacks that create frustration or defeat. In those moments, practice taking a pause before responding. Instead of relinquishing your aspirations, focus on pinpointing one manageable step forward. This intentional shift transforms energy into problem-solving and keeps you anchored to your objectives.

Developing resilience and encouraging growth requires self-awareness. This means being aware of your emotions as they happen, helping you respond thoughtfully instead of reacting impulsively. Techniques like deep breathing, visualization, or cognitive reframing are invaluable in calming responses to triggers. Each instance you choose to respond constructively strengthens your resilience, gradually making it easier to push through challenges. If you find yourself anxious in a high-pressure situation, employing deep breaths, visualizing a successful outcome, and reframing the challenge as an opportunity to demonstrate your capabilities can significantly alleviate stress. In the middle of challenging situations, sometimes it's better to count to ten and understand what you're feeling and why before giving your feedback. This pause allows you to harness clarity from emotions that might otherwise cloud your judgment. Not only does this helps you to provide better feedback that is both insightful and constructive, but it also strengthens your capacity to engage in meaningful and effective dialogues. By taking a moment to reflect, you ensure that your responses align with your long-term goals and maintain focus on navigating obstacles with poise and confidence. Over time, this practiced approach not only builds confidence but also strengthens your emotional resilience. Admittedly, maintaining composure when emotions escalate has been challenging for me. It's important to prevent instinctive reactions from taking control and to ensure conversations and communication remain clear.

In conclusion, effectively recognizing and managing emotional triggers is key to long-term success. By gaining a better understanding of your emotional responses, you equip yourself to handle life's challenges with confidence. Every step you take to identify and adjust your reactions to triggers builds resilience, supporting your journey toward change. This not only fosters personal growth but also inspires others, creating a wave of positive influence. By mastering this skill, you prepare yourself to face life's challenges with strength and assurance, turning your journey into a story of success.

Strengthening Emotional Intelligence

Developing emotional intelligence is one important component in building resilience and achieving sustained success. This process begins with enhancing self-awareness, which serves as the very foundation of emotional intelligence. By regularly tuning into your emotions, you gain a deeper understanding of your motivations and reactions across different situations. Cultivating self-awareness is a move that allows you to identify recurring emotional patterns, whether in work challenges or interpersonal conflicts, paving the way for more deliberate decision-making. When overwhelmed by stress during project deadlines, recognizing this pattern can be transformative. Instead of panicking, reminding yourself that stress can be a catalyst for enhanced focus and productivity can help manage your response more effectively, aligning your actions with your long-term goals. While stress is often perceived as negative, it's empowering to realize that it can also serve as a positive force when managed wisely with emotional intelligence. By shifting your perspective, you can transform stress into a motivator, driving you toward achieving your objectives. Understanding and reframing stress in this way enhances clarity and decision-making. Changing long-standing behaviours is tough but essential for building resilience. It requires conscious effort and practice to change responses that may hold you back. By identifying and changing these habits, you empower yourself to turn obstacles into opportunities, aligning your actions with your goals and boosting personal and professional growth.

In tandem with self-awareness, practicing empathy significantly enhances your interpersonal skills. Empathy allows you to see situations from others' perspectives, improving your ability to communicate and connect authentically. Compassionate responses, supported by empathy, build trust and collaboration, both of which are essential for nurturing robust personal and professional relationships. Cultivating a goal-oriented and resilient mindset is crucial, but it's just as important to keep empathy in the mix for well-rounded growth. When you consider the perspectives and needs of those around you, you create a balanced approach that not only moves you forward but also strengthens the community and support system you rely on. On the other hand, it is important to balance empathy with boundaries to avoid emotional overextension and maintain your well-being. Consider the scenario where a colleague is struggling with a task. Instead of merely offering advice, ask questions that demonstrate your understanding of their challenges. This approach not only builds relationships but is also beneficial for fostering a culture of open communication, which is critical for any successful team dynamic. We all know that it's not always easy, but it shouldn't be. That's why we are here to learn. Do not consider it as manipulation but more about learning and educating yourself. It's not all about making yourself better. It's also about helping others in their journey. You might not be the only one struggling. By creating a supportive environment where everyone feels empowered to grow, we craft a culture of mutual respect and continual improvement. When we embrace learning together, we boost our skills and lift up those around us.

Moreover, strengthening your emotional regulation skills is paramount to managing your responses under pressure, directly impacting your capacity to stay calm and focused during challenges. The ability to regulate your emotions equips you to handle difficult situations with resilience, ultimately enhancing your ability to recover from setbacks. Because you can be sure that there will be setbacks, remember that life is not always dancing on roses. Implementing simple techniques like deep breathing, reframing situations, or pausing before reacting can significantly aid in managing emotions constructively. These practices act as instruments to handle tense situations with calmness and foresight. Just as a well-regulated response can prevent escalations, it also ensures that your actions remain aligned with your goals—a key aspect of personal and professional success.

The journey to enhancing emotional intelligence is both dynamic and empowering, providing valuable insights and benefits. By incorporating these practices into your everyday life, you not only boost your immediate emotional resilience but also build a strong foundation for future successes. As you become more aware of your emotions, practice empathy intentionally, and improve your emotional control techniques, you move closer to a life filled with balanced, insightful, and empowering experiences. Each proactive step and intentional decision strengthen your ability to not only endure challenges but to thrive beyond them, creating a narrative of lasting success and meaningful change. From self-awareness to empathy and regulation, each aspect of emotional intelligence enriches your journey, promoting personal growth and inspiring those around you in a wave of positive transformation.

Cultivating a Positive, Resilient Mindset

Cultivating a positive, resilient mindset is an inspiring journey that underpins your drive to improve and achieve meaningful goals. At its core, embracing optimism acts as a powerful catalyst for growth. By viewing challenges as valuable opportunities to develop new skills and deepen your understanding, you reinforce resilience and fuel your drive to progress. This mindset shift begins with replacing limiting thoughts with encouraging, growth-oriented self-talk that keeps you motivated and focused on improvement. Optimism, therefore, is not merely looking on the bright side; it is about focusing on the potential gains from each experience, which in turn propels personal and professional growth through intentional, positive thinking. Resilience can develop from negative experiences, but relying only on negativity as motivation can be risky. It might drive you for a while, but it often lacks the endurance needed for long-term success and fulfilment. Recognizing feelings of doubt or inadequacy can motivate you, but they might also lead you off course if not balanced with positivity. So, it's important to understand the role of negativity, but make sure to balance it with positive energy for lasting resilience. That's why I prefer to rely on positivity as the guiding force for a resilient mindset.

One effective approach is incorporating gratitude into your routine, which bolsters your commitment to self-improvement and strengthens emotional resilience. Recognizing even small advancements enhances your dedication and growth potential. Gratitude can be developed not only for successes but also for the lessons and growth gained from tackling challenges. Establishing a daily gratitude practice – such as reflecting at the end of each day and noting three things you learned, or steps taken towards your goals – can be transformative. This simple yet impactful exercise directs your focus on achievements, emphasizing that each day you are progressing toward becoming the person you wish to be. Once again, I acknowledge that it may seem foolish, but have you tried it? I suspect you have not, and perhaps that is the reason you are seeking a new approach to behaviour and thought. Embracing gratitude and positivity may appear simplistic, yet they constitute the foundation for genuine resilience.

Building confidence through intentional action complements the process of mindset cultivation. When you set and achieve goals that align with your growth aspirations, you strengthen your confidence by offering clear evidence of your progress. This approach encourages focusing on growth rather than perfection, celebrating advancements rather than seeking flawless outcomes. Such a mindset not only supports resilience but also drives you to persevere amid challenges. Regularly reflecting on past achievements reinforces your belief in your abilities and boosts your confidence to tackle new challenges and further your success. For instance, if a new responsibility feels intimidating, recalling similar challenges you have already conquered can remind you of your capability and fortify your confidence to face what lies ahead. I encourage you to reflect on your journey and recognize that each experience, whether perceived as a success or a lesson, has equipped you with the resilience and skills needed to thrive in new endeavours. At least it works for me, so why not for you?

When integrated, these practices form a strong framework for developing a resilient and positive mindset that drives ongoing growth and success. The combination of optimism, gratitude, and confidence-building shapes a mental environment where challenges become opportunities, gratitude highlights progress, and confidence energizes you to pursue goals with determination. This intentional journey, crafted with strategic and insightful practices, not only enhances your personal growth but also inspires those around you, sparking a chain reaction of positive change. By incorporating these principles into daily life, you're not just building emotional resilience; you're laying the groundwork for lasting change and sustained success. As you advance with a fortified mindset, keep in mind that every positive thought, moment of gratitude, and confident step brings you closer to your goals, creating a story of ongoing improvement and lasting excellence.

7

Maintaining Momentum and Overcoming Setbacks

Momentum in resilience is like a powerful wave that drives you forward through life's challenges and achievements. It amplifies your past successes, and the lessons learned from setbacks, maintaining your drive as you face future adversities. Building momentum requires a mix of consistency and flexibility; consistency strengthens habits that boost resilience, while flexibility helps you adapt to unexpected situations. This momentum thrives on understanding your inner strengths and maintaining a clear focus on your goals. In the pursuit of progress and self-enhancement, maintaining momentum and overcoming setbacks are skills that define one's journey towards success. Life's path is often fraught with obstacles that demand persistence and an unwavering will. Embodying the principles of resilience and determination, this chapter explores the foundational elements necessary for sustaining progress: setting up systems for continuous advancement, staying motivated during challenging periods, and harnessing mental resilience.

The first key to enduring success is establishing a robust system designed to support ongoing progress. Such systems layer a framework of accountability and continual improvement, providing structure amidst the chaos of daily life. By setting clear goals, creating actionable plans, and instituting mechanisms for regular review and adjustment, you lay the groundwork for steady advancement. The system you create acts as an anchor, ensuring that even when passion dips, the structured routine keeps you moving forward. It's your blueprint for life, guiding you back to your path whenever you veer off course, allowing your journey to be defined not by the occasional stumble but by consistent steps forward.

It's equally important to remain motivated during challenging times. Difficult moments test our determination and can often risk hinder our progress. IIn these times, fostering intrinsic motivation, a strong personal drive based on your values and long-term goals, can help sustain you. Aligning your actions with your core motivations taps into an inner reserve of willpower, helping you persevere when external motivators weaken. Furthermore, by dividing larger goals into smaller, actionable steps and celebrating small wins, you can renew your enthusiasm and turn intimidating tasks into manageable challenges. This step-by-step approach not only sustains momentum but also fosters a sense of accomplishment that drives you forward.

Harnessing mental resilience is the third cornerstone of enduring progress. Resilience empowers you pass through the gray stone, utilizing setbacks as a catalyst for growth rather than reasons for retreat. By developing a resilient mindset, you gain the ability to adapt quickly to change, learn from failures, and redefine obstacles as opportunities for innovation and self-discovery. Cultivating resilience starts with self-awareness – understanding your triggers, strengths, and weaknesses – and builds through continual practice of positive thinking, stress management, and emotional regulation. By challenging negative thoughts and nurturing a sense of hopefulness, you equip yourself with the mental tools necessary to weather any storm.

Together, these elements create a powerful trio that supports steady progress. Strategically implementing systems ensures a consistent path forward; motivation acts as the driving force during challenging times; and resilience strengthens you against inevitable obstacles. By combining these principles, you establish a cycle of growth where each advancement builds on the last, creating a self-sustaining loop of success. This chapter will explore these key components further, providing practical strategies to improve your journey towards success. Embrace this path with confidence and determination, for the power to overcome setbacks lies in your own will. Each challenge you overcome becomes proof of your resilience, showing not just your ability to endure life's challenges but to triumph over them with determination and poise.

Setting Up a System for Continuous Progress

Creating a system for continuous progress helps you to maintain momentum in the pursuit of long-term goals. Like mentioned already before, establishing routines plays a pivotal role in this system by fostering a disciplined approach to work and personal development. By incorporating daily and weekly habits, such as setting aside dedicated time each morning or week for goal-focused activities, individuals can ensure steady progress without feeling overwhelmed. It is essential to prioritize tasks that have a significant impact on your overarching goals, ensuring that every action taken directly contributes to your vision. We have already discussed setting up systems to cover important topics daily, allowing you to incrementally advance your goals. To achieve this, knowing what to focus on is essential. Prioritizing tasks is crucial for maintaining continuous progress. Successful individuals often use methods like the Eisenhower Box or the ABC prioritization technique to categorize tasks by urgency and importance. By focusing on the top priorities and dedicating efforts to these tasks until they are completed, one can ensure steady advancement before tackling additional responsibilities. Begin by clearly defining and prioritizing your tasks, then allocate time for each task according to its level of priority to ensure focused and strategic progress.

Evaluating progress regularly is another critical component of a successful system. Setting up frequent check-ins, whether weekly or monthly, allows you to review what you have accomplished, assess obstacles, and make necessary adjustments to stay aligned with your goals. Tracking key milestones and outcomes can reinforce resilience, as it clearly demonstrates how each effort brings you closer to your desired outcomes. This reflection also encourages adaptability – a crucial aspect of resilience – by facilitating adjustments to your course without losing sight of your end goal. Successful individuals often set aside time at the end of each week to review their progress towards personal goals. They assess their accomplishments and identify any hurdles faced, using this reflection to adjust their strategies and priorities for the upcoming week. By doing so, they ensure continuous alignment with their objectives and maintain forward momentum. They also seek feedback from mentors or peers to gain new insights and perspectives. This disciplined approach to planning and self-evaluation fosters consistent growth and achievement. If you're already thriving and tracking progress online, you might think these steps aren't necessary. Still, doing a quarterly review is worth it just to make sure you're not veering off course and to tweak things if needed.

Drawing strength from your progress and building motivation through resilience is the final link in maintaining an effective system for continuous progress. Regularly reflecting on how your resilience has developed through the maintenance of routines and the overcoming of challenges serves as proof of your capacity to handle future obstacles. Each small success acts as a source of strength, validating that steady, consistent efforts yield tangible results. Taking pride in personal growth and progress not only becomes a motivational tool in itself but also makes it easier to remain driven when faced with difficulties. For instance, after a month of adhering to your routines, reviewing your accomplishments and recognizing mindset shifts can significantly boost your motivation. This reflection highlights the strength and growth that arise from routine and consistency, reinforcing the notion that with persistence, any challenge can be overcome. Just like being on a diet, when you see your progress, it fuels your motivation to keep going. Yet, resilience becomes crucial when progress momentarily stalls. When you push through these periods, you can pat yourself on the back and appreciate the mental strength you've developed.

Ultimately, establishing a simple system with a focus on routine creation, progress evaluation, and resilience cultivation paves the way for sustainable success. The strategic layering of actions and reflections ensures that momentum is not only maintained but also enhanced with every step forward. Engaging in this process with a sense of empowerment and strategic insight transforms the pursuit of goals into a journey, characterized by resilience, steady growth, and commitment to personal and professional excellence.

Staying Motivated During Tough Times

If this journey were easy, everyone would be achieving their goals effortlessly, and the insights provided by this book would not hold the transformative power they do today. Staying motivated during tough times is a fundamental aspect of maintaining momentum and overcoming setbacks, especially when pursuing personal goals. To achieve lasting change, it's essential to accept that the process requires time and commitment. This journey is gradual, and it's crucial to acknowledge that slow progress is a normal part of building new habits and working toward meaningful goals. Setting realistic expectations about the pace of change is vital to nurturing resilience. It's important to embrace the understanding that change doesn't happen overnight and the introduction of new habits takes several weeks. This viewpoint can ease frustration and highlight the value of patience and persistence. By dedicating yourself to long-term goals and seeing each small step as part of a bigger journey, you lay the groundwork for lasting success. For example, if you're striving toward a significant career goal, remembering that setbacks and gradual progress are natural parts of this journey can reinforce your commitment to stay the course. Remember, setbacks are a natural part of the journey, and some events may be beyond your control. Embrace resilience as a vital skill for both personal and professional growth. Approach challenges as opportunities for development and keep moving forward with confidence and purpose. Each small improvement along the way is a testament to your dedication and resilience.

Amidst challenges, finding meaning in your journey is crucial. Reconnecting with your core reasons for pursuing your goals helps when motivation dips. This deep sense of purpose fuels your resilience, reminding you why you chose this path. Difficult times present growth opportunities and recognizing that over-coming them is vital for personal development is empowering. Rather than focusing only on perfect results, it's important to celebrate small progress. Every milestone, no matter how small, reflects your dedication and resilience. When life feels overwhelming and knocks you down, take a moment to assess the situation calmly. Remember, you're not alone in feeling this way; everyone experiences setbacks. Embrace change as a powerful ally and harness your willpower to navigate through challenges, step by step. Life's unpredictability often catches us off guard, especially in a world that tends to shield us from adversity. When challenges arise, they might initially seem overwhelming, but cultivating mental toughness is crucial for breaking through barriers. Embrace the journey of developing resilience, recognizing that each obstacle is an opportunity to build strength and navigate life's complexities with greater confidence.

Especially at the start of the journey, harnessing small rewards and positive reinforcement enhances your ability to maintain motivation during challenging times. Celebrating small victo-ries boosts morale, with each achievement serving as positive reinforcement for your efforts, strengthening both motivation and resilience. Establishing a system of small rewards to acknowledge your dedication can significantly enhance your commitment to progress. Equally important is practicing self-compassion in the face of setbacks. Self-kindness fortifies resilience, encouraging you to stay motivated in the face of challenges. For example, whenever you achieve a milestone, no matter how small, reward yourself meaningfully. This could be a short break or a personal reward. Celebrating these achievements reinforces your resilience and determination, ensuring you continue advancing despite challenges. By adopting this comprehensive approach, you cultivate a framework for maintaining motivation during tough times, ensuring each step forward contributes to sustained momentum and growth.

Harnessing Mental Resilience to Push Forward

Harnessing mental resilience to push forward is essential in transforming aspirations into tangible achievements. This journey demands tapping into the power of will, dedication, and desire to grow and excel. Central to this transformation is the understanding that nothing of true value comes without persistent hard work and unwavering commitment. By aligning your goals with a profound and personal sense of purpose, you create an unstoppable force capable of propelling you forward, even when faced with life's most rigorous challenges. It's through this connection to a deep internal drive that one's willpower becomes an indomitable force, enabling you to maintain focus not only on immediate hurdles but also on the lasting impacts your objectives will have. Revisiting your personal "why" regularly is a strategy that builds mental fortitude, ensuring your dedication remains steadfast despite the roadblocks encountered. The aspiration to advance in your career can be fueled by motivations such as personal growth, financial security, or achieving a fulfilling lifestyle. This connection anchors your willpower, reinforcing both resolve and persistence. When doubt obscures my direction, I pause to reassess and reflect on the fundamental reasons for my goals, gaining clarity through this introspection. While questioning my decisions can feel unsettling, this process revitalizes my motivation, allowing me to move forward with renewed determination and focus.

Moreover, embracing hard work as an integral part of the mastery journey enhances resilience and invigorates the drive to succeed. This perspective allows you to see each challenge and setback as valuable opportunities for growth, reminding yourself that the struggle is a natural component of the success equation. Persistence through discomfort is crucial, for it's through enduring these trials that strength and skill accrue, paving the way for lasting improvement. Consider the process of mastering a new skill: each difficulty encountered and overcome contributes to your progress. The dedication to continued practice, despite hardship, gradually refines your abilities, making you more skilled and powerful as time goes on. This mindset encourages you to view every obstacle as a stepping stone, a defining moment in your ongoing developmental journey. There have been times when I've thought, "Not this again!" Yet it is the refusal to give up that drives me forward, reminding me that I can persevere if I put everything into play and approach challenges strategically. My willpower and desire have been pivotal in overcoming obstacles, igniting the determination needed to succeed.

Another foundational pillar in building mental resilience is the cultivation of self-discipline and consistency. Establishing, and adhering to, a structured routine reinforces the regularity necessary for genuine progress over time. By holding yourself accountable to your goals and focusing on intrinsic motivation instead of waiting for external validation, you strengthen your path forward. This internal framework is crucial for building resilience, as it is developed through daily dedication to your objectives. Each small success on this journey confirms both your progress and inner strength. Committing to a structured daily routine, like setting aside time each day to improve a skill or complete a task, fosters the self-discipline necessary to enhance resilience. Over time, this sense of purpose and commitment turns each milestone into a significant achievement, with each small step serving as proof of your lasting determination and growth potential. By thoughtfully combining these elements— purpose, hard work, and discipline—you create a solid foundation for a resilient approach to life's challenges, ensuring that you not only maintain momentum but also continue advancing toward your most valued goals.

8

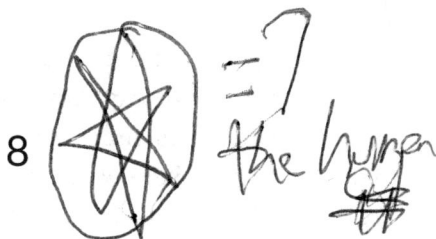

Integrating Resilience into Daily Life for Ongoing Success

As we begin the final chapter of our transformative journey, we focus on integrating resilience into our daily lives for lasting success. This chapter provides strategies to align purpose, commitment, and influence, forming the foundation for a life of strong perseverance. We explore how creating a resilient daily routine can significantly impact your life, setting the stage for both immediate accomplishments and long-term fulfilment. As mentioned, many times before a key aspect of building a resilient life is establishing a consistent and purposeful daily routine. The journey toward achieving your goals and cultivating resilience demands unwavering daily effort; without dedicating yourself each day, resilience and progress remain elusive dreams rather than attainable realities. Just as strength is built through consistent training, resilience is forged through persistent commitment to your objectives, transforming aspirations into concrete achievements. By organizing your daily activities systematically, you create a reliable structure that aligns with your goals and values. This approach helps you anticipate challenges while maintaining a resilient response. Developing a routine that focuses on mental and physical well-being, sets achievable goals, and encourages continuous learning is fundamental to resilience. It involves taking deliberate steps every day to cultivate the habits and mindsets necessary for thriving, providing a solid foundation for resilience to grow and lead you to success.

Transitioning from the daily to the monumental, we focus on the long-term strategies essential for sustained resilience. These strategies involve cultivating a mindset that is both adaptive and forward-thinking, crucial for navigating the complexities. Emphasizing flexibility, optimism, and strategic planning encourages us to view setbacks as opportunities for growth rather than insurmountable obstacles. By engaging in practices such as reflective journaling, lifelong learning, and embracing change, you empower yourself to remain resilient in the face of life's ebb and flow. These practices not only support sustained success but also act as a strategic roadmap for achieving your long-term aspirations with confidence and grace.

Equally important as nurturing your inner resilience is the influence it exerts on those around you. As you transform, your resilience becomes a beacon of inspiration to others, demonstrating the power of unwavering conviction and action. By sharing your journey, experiences, and insights, you not only reinforce your own resilience but also pave the way for others to cultivate theirs. Leading by example through your steadfast dedication and adaptability, you create an environment that values and encourages resilience. This shared influence amplifies the effect of your resilience, motivating those who observe your journey to follow their paths with renewed energy.

By focusing on these three key components, you can create a lasting foundation of resilience in your life and influence others positively. Incorporate these methods: establish a strong daily routine, develop long-term strategies, and motivate those around you. Each serve as a crucial step toward achieving the ongoing success you desire. Embracing this journey is a significant advance. Let's explore the following sections that delve into these principles, providing valuable insights and practical strategies to strengthen your resilience, ensuring it becomes a driving force in your success.

Building a Resilient Daily Routine

Creating a resilient daily routine is your launchpad for achieving personal goals with sustained vitality and determination. By implementing structured habits that drive daily progress, you transform everyday actions into building blocks for success. A well-structured daily schedule should prioritize actions that are directly aligned with your objectives, breaking down larger tasks into manageable steps. This approach ensures that each day is purposefully geared toward forward momentum. Let's be real for a moment. It might feel a bit silly, but a lot of us start our day without a clear idea of what we want to achieve. We're just drifting through each day. And let's face it, not every day will go perfectly. You can't operate like a robot — common sense and a bit of flexibility are essential. Still, remember that consistency is crucial to making progress. Consistency in your habits builds resilience, as it necessitates mental strength and commitment, even when faced with challenges. On challenging days, focusing on the process rather than immediate results fosters patience and persistence, underscoring the belief that steady actions breed long-term growth. For instance, initiating your day with a morning ritual can set a resilient tone; begin by reviewing your goals, setting priorities, and engaging in a grounding activity to center your thoughts. If your current routine isn't sparking the results you crave, it might be time to shake things up and try something fresh that truly aligns with your goals. This isn't about rigid adherence; it's about exploring what works best for you. Be proactive in your approach – experiment, adapt, and don't hesitate to pivot when necessary. Remember, with genuine desire and commitment, you'll carve out a path to the success you envision.

Incorporating practices for mental and physical renewal throughout the day further solidifies resilience. Allocate time weekly to reflect on what has been achieved, overcome, and learned, constructing mental resilience through constructive processing of challenges. Physical activity serves as a cornerstone for developing resilience, as it strengthens the body and aids in stress management. Introducing regular exercise or short, intentional movement breaks within your routine reinforces your resolve, both physically and mentally. Additionally, mindfulness or breathing exercises are important for maintaining mental clarity and emotional balance, sustaining your fortitude as you navigate daily tasks. Consider incorporating a quick midday check-in to reflect on the morning's achievements, indulge in mindful breathing, and recharge for the tasks that lie ahead. Feeling like you're dashing through the day with no clear direction can be overwhelming, almost like running around like a headless chicken. It's crucial to hit the pause button between tasks. These little breaks aren't just time-outs; they're valuable opportunities to reset your focus and clarify your next move. So, take a moment, breathe, and realign yourself. You'll find that a brief reflection can make a huge difference in steering your day where you truly want it to go.

Committing to self-care and retaining flexibility within this structured routine is critical for lasting resilience. Self-care acts as a foundational pillar, offering the energy and focus required to persevere and maintain consistent progress. Equally important is injecting flexibility into your routine, recognizing that the essence of resilience lies not just in consistency, but in the capacity to adapt to unforeseen changes while pursuing your goals. This balance between structure and adaptability empowers you to navigate the ups and downs of life with confidence. Celebrating small wins along the way boost motivation, affirming the efficacy of your perseverance. To conclude your day, take the time to reflect on specific achievements, no matter how small, and celebrate them as milestones on your resilience journey. This acknowledgment reinforces your commitment to growth and excites your purposeful advancement. Resilience is a powerful skill that, like a muscle, can be trained and strengthened. However, it also requires rest to recover effectively. The more you nurture it, the quicker it rebounds, leading to incremental growth and development.

These strategies represent a strong, process-focused approach to daily life that builds resilience and boosts both mental and physical strength in achieving personal goals. By organizing your routine around intentional, small actions that contribute to a bigger picture, you establish a resilient foundation that supports current objectives and develops the strength needed for continuous success.

Long-Term Resilience Strategies for Sustained Success

In the journey to build resilience into everyday life, adopting a growth mindset is crucial for lasting success. This mindset promotes the idea that each accomplished goal is not the end but a step towards further progress. By seeing things this way, you develop mental resilience, allowing you to view challenges as chances for growth. This understanding fuels the inner strength needed to keep pushing limits, aiding both personal and professional growth. Once a challenging project is completed, instead of resting on your achievements, use that energy to aim for a more ambitious goal, like mastering a related skill or entering a leadership role, using resilience as a driving force for advancement. They say that development ends with satisfaction, and yes, that's partly true, but each accomplishment is also a launchpad for your next big venture. So, why not tackle the next challenge with the excitement and motivation you've earned from previous successes? Embrace the next steps with an open mind, eager heart, and willingness to grow even more. Remember, the energy you've gained is your most powerful tool to get you forward.

Regularly reassessing and adjusting long-term goals strengthens your resilience and supports ongoing success. Taking time to evaluate your progress and future direction allows for a flexible approach that matches your changing aspirations. By adapting to new circumstances while staying focused on your goals, you embody resilient growth. This flexibility ensures that you remain grounded in purpose, even when facing setbacks Trusting yourself can be complex, especially when hindsight makes you question past decisions. It's natural to think you might know better now, yet it's

crucial to remember those choices were made with care and consideration. When deciding on your future, take your time, think deeply, and plan thoroughly so that future you can confidently uphold those decisions. However, if circumstances shift and necessitate a change, approach it with the same level of thoughtfulness and dedication. Your adaptability can be a powerful asset, ensuring resilience even as environments shift. The same kind of persistence should be used when you achieve a goal: reflect on the journey, review your progress, and refine your next steps. Aligning your goals with your development and new opportunities reinforces resilience and keeps you true to your core purpose.

Furthermore, building habits that align closely with your long-term goals is vital for sustaining a strong and purposeful perspective. These habits create a framework where each action underpins your larger aspirations, ensuring that resilience is not an isolated trait but an integral part of your routine. Leveraging each achievement as a stepping stone to keep progressing, you derive motivation from accomplishments, recognizing them as tangible evidence of what's possible through resilience. For instance, upon reaching a professional milestone, you might set a personal challenge, such as acquiring a new skill that complements your career goals. This continuous cycle of setting new, ambitious aims keeps the resilient mindset engaged, consistently thriving on growth, and guiding you towards greater heights.

By using these strategies, you're not just setting a series of small goals; you're creating a resilient life plan that actively shapes a strong future. Each goal acts as both an endpoint and a fresh start, paving the way to a more fulfilling and empowered life. With this approach, setbacks become learning opportunities, and successes serve as stepping stones for further exploration. The habit of continuous growth, adaptation, and purposeful progress becomes second nature, making resilience a guiding force that ensures persistent success, regardless of the challenges faced.

Inspiring Others Through Your Resilience

Inspiring others through your resilience is not only a generous act but a powerful tool to create lasting change and unity. Sharing your journey openly with others can spark motivation and provide a realistic perspective on the resilience journey. By opening about the challenges you've faced and the triumphs you've celebrated, you demonstrate that setbacks are an integral part of growth. This transparency shows those around you that resilience is achievable and not merely an abstract concept. By sharing how you've overcome obstacles, you can empower others to embark on their own paths, highlighting that resilience isn't about never stumbling but about learning and growing stronger from each experience. You might for instance recount a time when resilience helped you navigate a significant challenge, using your story to inspire others to adopt similar strategies in their lives and remind them that every small success is a victory. I've noticed that people close to me can see my growth and way of operating, even when I haven't mentioned it, and it often inspires those ready for change. This transformation seems to speak for itself, encouraging others to start their own journeys, at least the ones who are ready for it. But be mindful that some might not be ready and could try to hold you back but don't let that dim your progress.

Building a supportive community of resilient individuals

enhances not only your personal growth but also enriches the journey of everyone involved. Creating an environment that prioritizes mutual support enables community members to build resilience. In this space, open communication is invaluable – everyone benefits from sharing struggles and achievements, thus learning from each other's experiences. This shared growth mindset becomes a foundation for resilience, encouraging everyone to celebrate progress and reinforcing a collective sense of accomplishment. An example might be organizing regular group check-ins, where people openly discuss their goals, setbacks, and breakthroughs, cultivating an atmosphere where resilience is a continuous cycle of support and encouragement. In essence, it's about spending quality time with our like-minded friends, exchanging experiences and uplifting one another in a supportive environment. Such gatherings build a collective resilience that is far stronger than any individual's.

Mentoring others to break through their own barriers is another powerful method of spreading resilience. Mentorship involves helping others to recognize and build upon their strengths, empowering them to face challenges with renewed confidence and courage. Mentoring does not only involve guidance but also sharing practical tools and techniques that can be used to develop resilience. Providing actionable steps and strategies allows individuals to effectively manage physical and mental barriers with purpose. By viewing resilience as a lifelong skill that grows with each encounter, you help others integrate it into their own lives. For instance, if someone is facing a difficult time, you might offer guidance on how to deconstruct large challenges into manageable steps, sharing your own resilience practices as a way to inspire determination and power of will.

Your support helps individuals see resilience not as a challenging trait to build but as an essential part of their personal growth journey.

Ultimately, the journey of resilience is far more meaningful when shared with others. Your resilience, expressed through storytelling, community building, or mentorship, serves as a beacon of hope and a catalyst for change, promoting growth and progress for everyone involved. Sharing these experiences not only boosts personal determination but also creates a ripple effect, inspiring others to build resilience in their own lives. This contributes to a network of empowered individuals. The mutual exchange of insights and encouragement ensures that resilience remains an active force, driving progress and crafting a future rich with growth and opportunities.

9

Conclusion

A s we reach the conclusion of "The Breakthrough Mindset: Cultivating Resilience for Personal Success," we reflect on the transformative power of resilience, a strength that goes beyond just endurance, allowing for success even in the face of challenges. Resilience empowers us to view obstacles not as obstacles but as invaluable stepping stones fostering growth. Through resilience, challenges become opportunities, catalyzing personal and professional success and cementing themselves as integral to our successes. Central to this journey is the adoption of a growth mindset. Shifting our perspective to see setbacks as opportunities for growth is pivotal for lasting change. Each experience and challenge help us develop adaptability and continuous growth. This mindset is crucial, as it enhances our ability to learn and improve with every obstacle we encounter, driving us toward our full potential.

Our readiness and commitment to change serve as another cornerstone of transformation. Real change begins with a decision – a readiness to embrace the journey with determination and commitment. Through resilience, we accept that meaningful progress requires determination and patience, embracing the process with an understanding that each step taken is vital to our personal evolution. The insights from this book empower us to take decisive action in pursuit of our ambitions. It highlights that our willpower, coupled with the readiness to act, is essential in transforming dreams into reality. The learning tools and strategies gathered here provide the framework necessary to strengthen our determination and convert challenges into avenues of empowerment and growth.

As we cultivate resilience within ourselves, we unlock an inner capacity that is not only transformative but also contagious, inspiring those around us. The narrative of resilience, threaded throughout this book, invites us to take the first steps on paths untraveled, guided by the fortitude we have built. Let your journey be characterized by the courage to pursue new possibilities, shaped by the resilient mindset that challenges are gateways to discovering our strength.

In conclusion, may these insights act as catalysts, guiding you towards a future built on resilience. Your journey is unique, and the shared experiences in these pages inspire you to face challenges with a refreshed sense of hope and purpose. Embrace the strength in knowing that your journey to success isn't limited by obstacles but is guided by the resilient spirit within you. And so, with every challenge faced and overcome, your breakthrough mindset grows stronger, leading you toward a landscape rich with opportunities and limitless potential. Seize these moments, ready to transform the ordinary into extraordinary outcomes, and continue to build a legacy of resilience, both individually and collectively.

Review

As we wrap up this journey, we encourage you to share your thoughts and experiences by leaving a review on Amazon. Your feedback is crucial helping us inspire more readers and refine our insights. Let's build a community focused on resilience and growth, where your voice enhances our shared story. Just click the link below and give you honest opinion:

https://www.amazon.com/review/create-review/listing?sin=B0DP35GSB1

10

References

Duckworth, A. (2016). *Grit: The power of passion and perseverance.* Scribner.

Dweck, C. S. (2006). *Mindset: The new psychology of success.* Ballantine Books.

Seligman, M. E. P. (2011). *Flourish: A visionary new understanding of happiness and well-being.* Free Press.

Frankl, V. E. (1946). *Man's search for meaning.* Beacon Press.

Brown, B. (2015). *Rising strong.* Spiegel & Grau.

Hanson, R. (2018). *Resilient: How to grow an unshakable core of calm, strength, and happiness.* Harmony.

Grant, A., & Sandberg, S. (2017). *Option B: Facing adversity, building resilience, and finding joy.* Knopf.

American Psychological Association. (2023). Building your resilience. Retrieved from https://www.apa.org/topics/resilience

Southwick, S. M., & Charney, D. S. (2012). *Resilience: The science of mastering life's greatest challenges.* Cambridge University Press.

Clear, J. (2018). *Atomic habits: An easy & proven way to build good habits & break bad ones.* Avery.

About the Author

Maxwell Renshaw is a writer dedicated to empowering readers to break free from limitations and achieve their full potential in business and life. With a background in sales leadership, business strategy, and psychology, he combines real-world expertise with practical insights to deliver actionable guidance. Maxwell's straightforward, no-nonsense style ensures readers walk away inspired and equipped to take meaningful action. When not writing, he explores new ideas, develops skills, and volunteers in winter sports, always driven by a passion for growth and resilience.

For more information and further reading, please visit the author's page on Amazon: www.amazon.com/author/maxwellrenshaw.

Made in the USA
Columbia, SC
06 February 2025